MC  .

SLAVERY

Human Trafficking and Other Forms of Slavery in Modern Times

Tyler Taplin

Contents

Introduction

Slavery is an institution that many thought had been left in history. The Abolition of Slavery Act was passed in 1833 in Great Britain and all men were declared free and equal on paper. This meant that no human being could be considered the property of another, an investment with a purchasing value. Under the legal framework of slavery there were obligations on the slave owner toward the enslaved such as clothing them, housing them, feeding them and there were restrictions on working hours; there was of course no freedom. 200 years on there is no country in the world, which legally acknowledges slavery as a legitimate practice, however, according to the Global Slavery Index, there is still an estimated 35.8

million people living in slavery around the world today.

This abundance is shocking to most that an archaic and hideous smear on our history can still be lingering in the shadows. What is more surprising is that it exists on every continent and in almost every country in the world today, including those with mature and sophisticated justice systems such as the United Kingdom.

It has been put forward that the practice of slavery never disappeared after its abolishment. Rather, it simply took on a clandestine form but did not take with it the checks and balances imposed on pre-abolition slave-owners. Therefore, there was no obligation to feed and clothe your slave, to provide them with adequate living quarters or decent hours and of course violence and threats of violence could be administered without outside knowledge. This new type of slavery meant a far smaller investment in capital and the return positively great. This is perhaps why it still manifests itself today, whether in the form of chattel slavery (a traditional form where a person is captured, born or sold into permanent servitude), contract slavery (persons are issued with a fake contract to make work seem legitimate) or debt-bondage (services are provided for a monetary loan, terms of these services are not defined and through false accounting and unfair penalties, the bonded labourer can never exit this situation). These forms of slavery further exhibit themselves through commercial sexual exploitation, forced labour, forced marriage and human trafficking. In fact human trafficking has been quoted as the third biggest illegal income generator in the world after drugs and arms. The combination of globalisation, poor socio-economic conditions and demand for cheap goods/services and contraband mean that there is no shortage of supply, demand is abundant and 'slaves' are typically transported from poorer to more prosperous regions, thus arriving in countries like the UK.

The faces of slavery are varied but those that are particularly vulnerable are women and children, as they make up the majority of the worlds poor. Therefore, understanding the gender dimension to this abhorrent practice is important to understand the causal factors of slavery, which include poverty and desperation. However, it is not just causes that need to be tackled in order to prevent slavery from taking shape in the first instance: the perpetrators of this crime should be adequately prosecuted and the victims protected. The

This book accordingly presents the key issues in understanding what this is, how it grows and how it can be prevented including what needs to be done to stamp slavery out once more.

Chapter 1
UNDERSTANDING MODERN DAY SLAVERY: KEY CONCEPTS AND ISSUES

What is modern day slavery?
Slavery is the subjugation of one person by another. In modern day it can take three broad forms:

1. Chattel slavery – most similar to traditional, pre-abolition slavery, where a person is captured, born or sold into permanent servitude. This is the least

.

common form of slavery in present day but is still reported in some parts of the world.

2. Contract slavery – 'employees' are offered a fake contract that makes work seem legitimate such as to work in a factory: once workers join their employer they find themselves in slavery like conditions such as being forced to work for no pay or as much to enable their subsistence and no freedom to leave the contract or the realm of the 'employer'.

3. Debt-bondage – services are provided in return for a loan, and the expectation is that the debtor will work off payment of the loan. However, the loaner does not define the terms of the service or loan and ensures that the debt is never paid through false accounting, unfair penalties or over inflated interest rates.

Force and Deception

Choice in an enslaved situation does not exist – victims are either forced or deceived into joining their aggressor. This can happen in the form of outright kidnapping, false advertising for jobs through adverts or trained recruiters, or with the complicity of the victims loved ones such as a boyfriend or parent who have been promised some monetary gain and who may or may not know the conditions within which the victim will be entering. Where a child or young person is concerned (a child is under the age of eighteen), force or deception is irrelevant – even if they walked away willingly with their aggressor, the latter can still be held liable for enslaving them.

Once in possession of the aggressor, whether they become aware that a job was not what it appeared to be or have been kidnapped, they are kept there by further forceful measures or coercion. This can mean they are locked up with physical guards watching over them. Victims may feel they are compelled to stay, as they believe they must pay off a debt. The use of mental tactics may also be used where the vulnerability of victims is preyed on. Victims may be fearful of approaching law enforcement for fear of being arrested; this is particularly true when victims are from outside of the country. Their passports may have been confiscated or threats of violence are used against them or their families. Actual violence and abuse is not an uncommon method used to enslave individuals and the process of "breaking" victims takes place through repetitive physical abuse such as beatings, rape and forcing a dependency on narcotics such as heroine. This breaks down the ability of victims to resist their aggressors, increasing their vulnerability and eliminating hope of escape from their prison.

Exploitation

The slave or victim is used to provide a service, cheaply sometimes with no pay and sometimes with little pay beyond that of subsistence i.e. to eat meagerly and be housed in often abhorrent conditions. The service may or may not be legal and the aggressor reaps the benefit, usually in the form of a monetary reward, without passing this on to the victim.

Causes of Modern Day Slavery

As will be covered in the next chapter, modern day slavery can encapsulate those seeking to migrate, in search of better opportunities or escaping ill conditions in their home country or area.

Poverty, leading to desperation, means that victims are susceptible to the lures of aggressors looking for vulnerable persons to exploit.

Conflict or disaster means that potential victims, for example, children, are often left orphaned or missing, leading them into the hands of traffickers or aggressors.

Lack of education can mean that victims are not often aware of the potential dangers of rogue recruiters or that their situation may lead them to exploitation.

Social oppression, for example among lower castes in some countries or persistent biases among certain socio-economic groups, mean that victims can find themselves inheriting the chains of the older generations. I.e. inheriting debt and entering cycles of debt bondage; or being involved in a cultural practice of prostitution under exploitative conditions.

Irregular legislation, as will be seen later on, can lead to loopholes that are exploited by aggressors, making it easier for them to enslave victims.

Weak rule of law and corruption allow for officials to be bribed or aggressors to go unquestioned. Victims are often treated as criminals instead of their aggressors, for example, in the use of commercial sexual exploitation and using slave labour to grow cannabis.

High demand for low cost goods and services and contraband keep conditions for slavery rife. This is known as "a race to the bottom" and is the result of globalisation.

Organised Crime
Slavery today is a crime and liable to criminal action. However, in addition, some forms of slavery

and the mode of operation in using slaves amounts to "organised crime" such as human trafficking (covered in chapter two). It involves a multi-layer operation, where the head of the unit is inaccessible. Associating slavery with organised crime can carry consequences. The term typically conjures up images of Mafias and enhances the fear of the victim: fear of reprisal against them or their family. This takes it out of the realm of ordinary criminal investigative procedures as real organised crime carries economic and political influence.

Corruption

The most desperate scenario comes when the state has a role to play in this set up by offering protection to gangs, capturing victims, receiving bribes and turning a blind eye, laws are unenforced and rogue honest officials are rendered helpless.

Numbers

The true number of slaves today will never be known due to the clandestine nature of modern day slavery. As with all crime, much activity goes undetected so any data that exists is inaccurate. When figures are formed, they start from a baseline of known cases, multiplied according to certain criteria to form an estimated guess. If one was to research into the phenomenon they would come across the same figures and quotes i.e. recycled data, without forming fresh investigations and therefore, invalid data is always present. What is also important to consider when reading calculated statistics for slavery is that many organisations will follow different definitions and encompass different types of slavery within their numbers, which explains where some differ. This places problems, whichever way it is looked at. Many argue that data possessed is not low because trafficking is clandestine; it is low because it does not exist or not to the extent that is often projected. Large numbers may be published to invoke an emotional response, mobilize public support or to increase police powers and resources.

Gender
Gender is an important dimension when trying to understand slavery. It is true that slaves take all forms, men, women and children but the majority of known victims are women and girls. Feminist theory has argued long about the lack of attention to the rights of women in drafting of human rights treaties, dating back to early state-making, while the public sphere of politics and power relations is dominated by men and the private sphere of family life is dominated by women. In the guise of

protecting the private sphere from state intervention, it can turn a blind eye to abuse experienced within the private sphere such as domestic violence, rape, battery and honour violence: abuses traditionally felt by women that naturalise gender inequalities. The physical and psychological abuse often experienced by female victims of slavery are not covered by the Universal Declaration of Human Rights and in many countries, abuses within the private sphere, where women are most vulnerable are not deemed a violation of human rights and states are not held accountable for their complicity in violations: gender inequalities are therefore, de-politicised.

Chapter 2 TYPES OF SLAVERY

Commercial Sexual Exploitation
Sexual exploitation is the most commonly
documented form of modern day slavery. Victims
will often be recruited under false pretences, such
as a promise of a job in a factory, as a waitress,
dancer or even stripper. However, once lured in
they are forced to participate in non-consensual
sexual acts against their will. This can include
prostitution, escort work or pornography. They are
often held against their will and forced using
physical and mental methods, including 'breaking
the victim down' through continuous acts of rape,
injecting them with drugs and increasing their
dependency on their aggressors. What is important

to understand here as well is that as the girls are acting against their will, they are often subjected to even more degrading acts that consensual sex workers may be unwilling to do thus increasing the appeal to their aggressors and fulfilling a demand. Women and underage girls are most susceptible to this type of abuse but men and boys are also affected.

Domestic Servitude
This type of exploitation overlaps with forced labour but occurs in private households, where victims are forced to carry out domestic chores. It is not uncommon for wealthier families and migrant families (in Western countries) to use live-in domestic servants and it is becoming an increasing trend. In particular, migrant families that come and settle in the UK are faced with the unfamiliarity of little/ no extended family as is present in their countries of origin and therefore help is brought over to assist with childcare and other domestic chores, which is cheaper than using childcare options or housekeeping that is UK based. This cheap source of labour often creeps into the category of slave-like practices when 'cheap' becomes little beyond sustaining themselves to keep alive. In fact pay is often withheld and domestic servants are kept confined within households. They have in the past been brought

over without their own passports as well and come as employees to work with specific employers. There has also been the trend of children coming over under the guise of private fostering arrangements or marriage (servile marriages). Abuse is easy to administer in these arrangements, as the victim feels isolated from what he/she knows: they may not know the language the local law enforcement system, they have no passport and they have no networks within foreign countries. As well as providing cheap or free labour and being restricted in their movements, victims are exploited by being made to work excessive hours with no free time and no privacy. As well as mental constraints, cases have been documented of physical abuse in such arrangements such as beatings, torture and rape.

Forced Labour
More research has been carried out on forced labour in recent years and more and more abhorrent cases are being unearthed. 'Sweatshops' have been running for hundreds of years, not just in far-flung places in the Far East or South Asia, but the UK has had its share of the legacy and this has been documented well into the 1970s notoriety being with the sweatshops of East London running on immigrants and their children. Prior to that, as early as the 19th century they operated in legality,

child labour under exploitative conditions in factories, agriculture or other services. Children lived in fear of their employers, injuries and deaths occurred without punity until measures were introduced to protect children. Cases of forced labour are still documented in industries such as fisheries, mining, tarmacking, agriculture, hospitality, food packaging and even prostitution Migrants, particularly illegal migrants, are vulnerable to this type of exploitation. In countries such as the UK, their precarious status makes them desperate and vulnerable to exploitative conditions and pay and are prepared to work for very low rates in hazardous conditions. Cases have been documented of employers using fear to increase outputs and make 'employees' work harder for longer hours. For example, verbal threats, physical abuse and threats to their families have been recorded as being used. In some cases this exploitation occurs after a victim has willingly accepted work but in others, victims are forced to partake from the outset. This type of exploitation is also closely linked to debt bondage and in order to pay off a debt, victims are forced to work but in actual fact their debt is never paid off partly because of their low wages and partly because these doubts are ever increasing – with food, rent expenses and inflated interest rates. They are subsequently 'owned' by their employer. Forced labour is on the continuous rise as demand for cheap goods and services have mounted, especially after the global recession. Instead of hiring long-term employees, short term contracting is used as and when required. Sub-contracting makes the supply chain harder to track, which is why this type of abuse can be easily administered.

Forced Marriage
This is a newly uncovered form of slavery. Servile marriages were mentioned, where migrants are brought over as spouses but are used for domestic chores. A forced marriage occurs when one or both parties have not freely agreed to the marriage. This is a large problem on its own but can lead to the woman (this is mostly a female issue; all child marriages are considered forced marriages) living in slavery like conditions. Power is controlled by either the mother-in-law or the husband. As well as endless household chores, women can be forced to work in family businesses with no pay or simply forced to have sex. Cases vary between forced marriage being a way of getting women into the country and women being first brought into the country (or transported out of it) to then be sold on into a marriage.

Criminal Exploitation

Criminal exploitation could be seen as another type of forced labour, except this type of labour is outright illegal and makes the victim more vulnerable. Children, in particular experience this type of abuse. Victims are controlled by criminal gangs, either large or small operations and are treated badly through some of the methods already discussed. They are forced into crimes such as cannabis cultivation, pick pocketing or begging against their will and even benefit fraud. They are never paid and if caught they are treated as criminals by the authorities. This type slavery, therefore, is the most unnoticed.

Human Trafficking
Modern day slavery and human trafficking go hand in hand. Victims of human trafficking are the definition of modern day slaves and they occur for all the purposes mentioned above. However, there is the added element of moving the victims so there is an idea that victims will be moved from one place to another. Different countries and sometimes different organisations within countries use different definitions. For example, some consider trafficking to be a practice that must happen across borders, therefore, country to country. Others believe that trafficking can happen within one country i.e. city to city. Then there is the idea that any type of movement will make it a

victim a trafficked victim, the victim just need to change hands. Another point of confusion is the difference between trafficking and smuggling. Smuggling is something that always happens between countries but actually it is different from trafficking because the smuggled 'victim' is there of their own free will.

As human trafficking often happens internationally, there is international law that sets a definition and even ways it should be prevented, prosecuted and methods of protection that should be afforded to the victim. This law is called the Palermo Protocol and describes the crime of human trafficking as having three parts:

- The movement/ transport of persons - the act.
- The use of force or deception and control - the means
- Benefit to a third party - the purpose.

Mostly, law enforcement is concerned with human trafficking because it has had connections to organised crime as mentioned previously. These may be small scale or large scale, even controlled by mafias. Despite their size they are organized in natures and involve several layers of operation under the head of the organization. Middlemen will organise the recruitment, transport, papers and sale of persons, perhaps all separate individuals. There may then be further roles as pimp or brothel owners in the case of sexual exploitation. These operations usually cannot occur without the co-operation of corrupt officials as well, either turning a blind eye or providing one of the steps such as forged paperwork.

Child Trafficking
Child trafficking is worth a separate mention here because although all of the above examples apply to children as well as adults, there are often special considerations that need to be afforded to children and they make up the largest percentage of victims. A difference is sometimes made between a child, someone under the age of 16, and a young person, someone under the age of 18. This occurs within single countries as well as between countries. Children are targets for traffickers because of their mental immaturity, respect for adults as authority figures and because they are also make up the largest proportion of those living in poverty. Children generally listen to adults so the adult always has an advantage. They are often recruited by someone they know well, a relative and sometimes the parents themselves. However, when families are involved they may not necessarily appreciate what lies in store for their child. Although many children have given their

consent to go with a trafficker, this is irrelevant for it to be a crime, where children are concerned. However, this is also the reason why there are few investigations for child trafficking and it goes on mostly unnoticed. Children are the most vulnerable group open to abuse: they are more likely to be deceived, less likely to come forward, less likely to know their rights and less likely to know where to obtain help.

The vulnerability of children also means that the impact on them is far greater and the trauma of the experiences they encounter can have lasting psychological effects.

Chapter 3 HOW DOES IT HAPPEN IN THE UK

When we think about modern day slavery, we imagine that it happens in foreign countries, but slavery still thrives in the UK today and usually happens through human trafficking from another country into the UK.

The Home Office, the UK Government Department responsible for immigration and crime, has a mechanism by which to identify potential victims of trafficking called the National Referral Mechanism.

Numbers

By the end of 2014, the number of potential trafficking victims had reached 2,340, a 34% increase on the year before.

But the official numbers of people referred to authorities are only a tip of the iceberg. The government's own estimates put the number of people in slavery in the UK at up to 13,000. Due to the clandestine nature of slavery, the true number is never really known.

Trends

The most common countries of origin have been from Albania, Nigeria and Vietnam. However there is a rise in people from Britain being trafficked throughout the country. The UK is actually the sixth most common country of origin. The most common form of slavery in this country is for the purpose of forced labour including domestic servitude and other forms of labour exploitation. Commercial sexual exploitation is also a very prominent purpose of slavery in the UK. There has also been a growing trend of victims being exploited for criminal purposes.

Methods of Operation

A child may claim to be from one country, while covering the fact they are from another: certain nationalities convey favourable asylum rights and officials may not be able to distinguish between them e.g. Pakistanis claim to have Afghan identities and Chinese children use South Korean documentation.

In many cases, the UK is not the final intended destination. For example, a notable country of origin for victims is West Africa, who are being trafficked to Italy to work as prostitutes. This route has become well known and virtually impossible to travel to directly without being stopped by the authorities, which is why the UK is used as a transit country. This route first gained its high profile in 1996 after an unaccompanied minor found at Gatwick airport, was taken into care and subsequently went missing. A study revealed that children would arrive unaccompanied at Gatwick Airport, claim asylum and then be taken into care due to their age by West Sussex Social Services. Once in care, they would find a way to contact their trafficker and one day they would suddenly go missing. The victims are pressured or coerced into doing what their trafficker asks through the use of voodoo, known as juju in West Africa. A curse is placed on the victim and they are told that it can only be lifted once a debt has been paid. If the debt goes unpaid, harm will be come to them or their family. That is why victims are willing to do whatever their aggressors ask.

Another trend is for West African children to live with strangers under private fostering arrangements and they are then used to claim benefit. A report in 2004 suggested that 10,000 West African children were living with strangers in the UK at the time. The most famous case in England is perhaps the one of Victoria Climbie. Her Aunt took Victoria Climbie from Cote D'Ivoire, to France and then the UK. This was all done on the pretext of her receiving a good education but she was actually used for her benefit allowance; she was tortured over a period of five months and then died as a result.

The Roma community has struggled to become accepted in any society within which they join and as a result of their persecutions, have come to depend on a life of crime. This is true in the UK as well. Cases have been cited of children being sent out by criminal gangs to beg and commit petty crime. Sometimes their own families are responsible for this under large joint family umbrellas as many Roma families are linked and spread across different boroughs.

Human trafficking from China is a well-organised, global operation. From China a harsh and arduous overland route is taken to Russia from where flights are taken onwards to the UK. Criminals use forged or stolen South Korean, Japanese or Malaysian passports in order to facilitate entry of persons into the UK. These nationalities are chosen because they do not need a visa to enter many of the European Union countries. Victims are also coached to deal with immigration and behaviour in order to avoid undue scrutiny by Border officials. In many cases, the victim needs to make an asylum claim in order to enter the UK. If they are children, they are taken into care. In many other cases, however, a more clandestine method has been used to smuggle victims into the UK. The appeal of the UK speaks to many of the poorer communities of China. They know there are many Mandarin and Cantonese speaking communities within the country and they can settle among them. As such, many approach traffickers directly, looking for better opportunities abroad or need little persuasion. However, they are then trapped into debt-bondage arrangements and situations of forced labour.

Since the military occupancy in Afghanistan and the rise in instability there, many Afghan nationals have sought refuge in the UK. The desperate need to leave has led many into the hands of traffickers and there are many agents available to facilitate this. If not claiming asylum, they use clandestine methods to enter and are used for forced labour and debt-bondage.

Cannabis hothouses have been recently uncovered. They use victims from Vietnam, usually children and young persons. Victims arrive using clandestine methods and false documentation and are immediately transferred to the factories. They may be aware of the work they are doing but as they are minors, exploited and restrained, they are victims. Unfortunately, instead of victims, the authorities tend to treat them as criminals. They are discovered during raids, are arrested and deported in many cases, receiving 12-42 months on detention orders or in youth offender's institutions. A trend amongst Eastern European originated trafficking is for traffickers to appear as boyfriends or friends. They are then coaxed to the UK to be with them and may involve the girl coming across on a tourist visa. They are then raped and forced into a world of sexual exploitation. There is a considerable amount of violent coercion involved in this method.

Slavery and trafficking, however is not just foreign born. It originates from within the UK borders also. The purpose of exploitation is mostly for sexual exploitation and mostly girls aged 11-17 years of age. The demographic of those vulnerable to exploitation and who become victims is not completely clear. Ethnicity in known cases varies greatly; cases include an equal proportion of girls living with their families as those that come from care, although 50% is an overrepresentation of those coming from care as they make up a far smaller proportion of the population. Victims are tricked under the guise of a loving relationship, this is known as grooming. There are four stages to this process. The first stage is to attract girls through gifts. The second stage is that of dependency they become dependent on their 'boyfriend' and are easily manipulated; the girl would be persuaded to cut off ties to loved ones. The third stage involves the 'boyfriend' taking over all aspects of the girl's life. Finally after complete domination they will do anything in order to please the 'boyfriend'. This includes having sex with strangers. The 'boyfriend' is usually part of a gang or 'peer group'. The use of the drugs is often used in order to heighten dependency. While under control, the relationship may have been transferred to an older member of a peer group and control is maintained through violence and threats.

Referrals

These clandestine methods and similarly to other criminal activities, means that the actual number o victims in slavery are not known. It is not until they are referred as a potential victim through the National Referral Mechanism that they become known. Referrals may happen after raids and officials identify the precarious situation around those they detain. Immigration officials may also recognise victims at the point they claim asylum. Child victims may be abandoned by their aggressors and taken to social services, by members of the same diaspora or others.

Demand

The reason why trafficking and slavery is so rife in the UK is because there is a demand, though this may not be conscious in the minds of the general public. The UK has a commercial sex industry, many families use domestic servants and benefit fraud is rife. Evidence exposes a demand for cheap labour and contraband encouraging further exploitation. Many argue that to tackle modern day slavery, it is important to tackle the demand side.

Chapter 4 CASE STUDIES

1.   In Wales, a man (Man A) had been brought to the UK to work on a local farm. He had been provided with accommodation and a wage, however, he did not receive any payslips. He noticed that deductions were being made from his wages but unfortunately the employment agency was not forthcoming for the reasons why. He was summarily dismissed and told to vacate his accommodation immediately.

2.   In 2008, an Indian man, Man B, approached a Citizens Advice Bureau (CAB) in Bridgend with a grievance about his employment company. He had received a work permit to enter the UK for a job with a food processing plant. He described to them workers from India were recruited to come to the

UK with the lure of work and conditions. However, once in the UK and working, they are forced to do many more hours or less hours and the pay was substantially lower. He stated that these workers were too frightened to stand up for themselves.

3.   Carmarthen CAB was approached by Man C, who was from Slovakia who worked via an agency for a company on a contract that started as a two month contract for fixed hours; but he soon discovered that he may not always be needed to come in for work everyday. The days he was not needed, he would not be getting paid and he was concerned that he would lose his job although turning up for work with this employer meant he would not have enough to live on.

4.   In 2012 Man D from Hungary came to the UK on advice from his friend that could earn £2,000 a month from working in a factory. He agreed to go. However, he travelled overland with three other men. His journey took two days, after which they arrived at a house. They were greeted by men, though the reception was not so friendly as his passport was confiscated, the men were held as prisoners and Man D was forced to forced to work. The job was in a factory as promised but was accompanied by three other jobs including selling mobile phones, distributing flyers working in a

pizza restaurant, stealing scrap metal and petrol, opening false bank accounts. The pay was meager, between £3 and £5 every week. During this time Man D became suicidal and fearful, he felt he could not escape. However, after some time, he noticed that his captors were not watching him so much. This was the opportunity he and the others needed to escape and they did so by jumping out of a window and running to the police. He became suicidal, but was too afraid to escape.

5.   Woman E fled from Uganda after she was detained, raped and tortured by Ugandan officials when reports of her having a same-sex relationship emerged. After eight months of this treatment, woman E became pregnant and she was released. She was told before she went to the UK that she could get well-paid work and could send this money back to Uganda for her daughter's education. Her arrangements were organised by an agent. Her daughter was left with a close family member and she went to work in the UK as a cleaner. She did actually go and work as a cleaner in the UK but she was told that because it cost money to bring her there, she would have to repay her debt. Woman D ended up having to clean every day and all day. She did not receive breaks and she was not paid. She was in actual fact treated as a slave – she had nothing to sleep on, was locked in

the basement, beaten, deprived of food and was not allowed to go outside. D's health really deteriorated from the lack of sunlight and malnutrition – her eyes were damaged from long exposure to sunlight and her limbs became stiff and painful. She eventually managed to escape on being discovered by a visitor who unlocked the basement door.

6.   Man F is from the UK but underwent a hard period after his mother died and became homeless. He was approached by two men while he was waiting for a bed at a shelter and they offered him work, accommodation, food and alcohol, playing on his vulnerabilities. He ended up sharing a damp caravan with three other men and forced to lay concrete slabs as well as other hard landscaping jobs from six a.m. to ten p.m. at night. He was never, paid was assaulted if he complained and was often made to sleep outside. He was then sold on, to a family for the price of £3,000 and was moved on to a different area. His suffering continued as he was forced to do many jobs such as cold calling for business, tarmacking etc. He did escape after four years and transport police were able to direct him to a homeless unit.

7.   Woman G left Sri Lanka to work for a family in Jordan, with whom she was badly mistreated.

The family travelled to many different countries and the UK was their next temporary destination. She found the job with this family through a 'friend' although she had to pay this friend for organising it. Her ordeal included sleeping in the living room, where she would not get any rest if people were coming home late; she worked 16 to 18 hours per day for £200 each month; her meals consisted of onions and potatoes unless there were leftovers; she was disrespected by all members of the family and was accused of taking missing food; she was verbally assaulted and unduly punished; she was not allowed days off. There was no escape for G as she did not have a visa and was refused any support for one by the family she worked for. She was allowed out of the house for food shopping at the supermarket only and it was there that she met anther domestic worker, who advised her about an NGO that could help her. This is how G escaped, with support from the NGO she was able to attain a visa, apply for indefinite leave to remain in the UK and get a UK residency, after which she was able to leave.

8.   Two men of Vietnamese origin, Man H and Man I came to the UK via a recruitment agent whom they paid £18,000. They were expecting to work in a hotel for £4.95 per hour but were in actual fact not paid at all. Their passports had been

confiscated at the beginning but they tried to protest at the hotel nevertheless. As a result their families were threatened. Despite the fear they must have been feeling, they managed to find a Vietnamese speaker who could interpret their issue with the Citizens Advice Bureau.

9.   Group J came from Poland to work in the UK. They were hired by an English recruitment agency, and interviewed in batches of ten in one of the major Polish cities. They were promised £4.50/hour, rent for £25 per week and lots of overtime in Southampton. They arrived in the middle of the night and were met by a middleman who took them to a house in Exeter. When they arrived at the house they were told to wait outside on the grass and witnessed a number of frightened Afghans throw their things into a black bin liners and then taken away in the van that brought group J to the house. None of the parties at the time spoke any English and therefore, no one could ask any questions nor answer any. Despite the promises, there was no work and no pay for the first week in Southampton where they were told they would be working. They were then sent to Devon to pack chicken in a Sainsbury's and were charged £40 per week (the restriction was £25 per week at the time for those on minimum wage). They were not hired by the company directly but

by a sub-contractor that was part of chain of sub-contractors, they did not even know the full name of the boss of the company. They lived in abysmal conditions: no furniture, soiled mattresses on the floor, heaps of rubbish and syringes with a bad stench. They slept on bare mattresses and were driven to their shifts, which were inhumanely long – 2am to 10pm. This group was controlled by what is known as a 'gangmaster'. They were threatened with eviction, loss of earnings and also with the police if they were to tell anyone about their situation. They felt helpless and intimidated and didn't feel they could tell anyone as they could not afford to register with the Home Office and so were already on the wrong side of the law; deductions would be made from their payslip without any explanation including extortionate tax although the tax office never received any of this. The workers eventually managed to escape their conditions after involvement of a union.

Chapter 5 HOW WE TACKLE MODERN DAY SLAVERY

Multi-faceted approach

When trying to understand trafficking, a number of frameworks can be considered: it is a moral problem a well as a criminal, labour, immigration, human rights and gender issue. The strategy adopted depends on the framework considered but must involve three strands: prevention, protection and prosecution.

Prevention

The best way to stop modern day slavery in the UK is to prevent it happening in the first place, deter people from exploiting individuals and deter individuals from situations of vulnerability and slavery.

It was mentioned that one of the root causes of slavery is desperation and poverty, which may come from living in countries with poor infrastructure, states that have been riddled with insecurity and from social exclusion i.e. coming from a race, class or caste that is systematically discriminated against. Therefore, it follows that to tackle modern day slavery, poverty should be tackled and therefore, we should invest in development programmes in countries acutely affected by such deep-rooted problems.
Modern day slavery can also be prevented through more awareness raising. Communities in countries of origin, that are vulnerable should be given more information on the dangers of going overseas or with recruitment agencies and provided with the warning signs. Better education will also prepare them for unscrupulous criminals and individuals that will try and take advantage of their situation. In the UK itself, emerging reports and increased media coverage has meant that there is growing awareness amongst the general public and if further advocacy is undertaken amongst community groups and schools then more and more cases will become referred and victims recovered before it is too late.

Less victims may be subjected to slavery as well if the demand side of trafficking was tackled. Targeting the purposes of slavery and getting tough on sexual exploitation and gangmasters, want for cheap goods etc, should work in tandem to supply-side prevention.

Protection

Part of any strategy to ensure the abolition of modern day slavery needs to ensure adequate protection exists for the victims of slavery and trafficking. Victims are often very fearful, traumatised and in ill-health. As well as a moral obligation and sense of humanity, victims in this state are not condusive to effective investigations. There should be standard working procedures to guarantee the safety of victims and if necessary protect their identity in order for them to testify against the perpetrators.

A number of facets go into the protection process. First victims must be identified. The risk is, however, is that very often victims are criminalized because they are usually irregular migrants. Therefore, frontline staff such as police, immigration officers, social workers etc should have mainstreamed training to recognize the signs of a potential trafficked victim including what questions to ask them, checklist and techniques. If a potential victim is found then they must be referred to the relevant organisation through a referral mechanism. After referral is where things become murky. It appears that victims tend to be repatriated and reintegrated to their country of origin. However, this has been a bone of contention as if trafficked victims, for example, are sent back to their country of origin then they are at risk of being re-trafficked. The reintegration programme can help in some circumstances where victims are provided with small loans to set up business or vocational training, but it is context specific. There could be more exploration of settling the victim in the country they have been trafficked to. Although there is a period where victims are provided with support, this usually happens in partnership with NGOs.

The UK's initiation of protecting victims involves the National Referral Mechanism, a framework designed to identify victims of human trafficking and refer them for protection and support. It affords them a minimum 45-day reflection and recovery period. Case owners will then decide whether they are indeed victims of human trafficking. The UK Human Trafficking Centre uses the NRM statistics to collect data about victims in order to build a clearer picture about the scope of human trafficking in the UK. The National Referral Mechanism fits guidelines from the European Union and the United Nations for identification of victims and is assign of progress in the last six years but it sill has its faults. Many organisations say that it does not adequately or systematically identify, assist and protect victims of trafficking. This problem is mostly evident because of the vast number illegal migrants and evidence shows that an irregular migration status will mean they are less likely to be identified as a trafficked victim than others for example, that are from a European Union country. They are subsequently deported rather than protected.

Prosecution

An effective anti-slavery strategy places great emphasis on ensuring effective prosecutions for those responsible for the crime of trafficking. Not only arrests and convections but also convictions commensurate with the gravity of the crime – large penalties need to be administered in order to deter criminals from entering into this depraved and barbaric endeavour.

However, most human trafficking or modern day slavery cases go unreported, because of the dark figure of crime and clandestine nature of it. Therefore, most perpetrators are never caught. The organized nature of the crime as mentioned earlier, that is its association with organized crime and mafias, also means that the heads of the organisation are hard to get to and never come anywhere near prosecution. In fact when prosecutions are made, it tends to be against petty middlemen. This is then linked to victim or witness protection and getting a victim who is brave enough to take the witness stand. Protection is therefore a key element in improving prosecution records.

Large penalties are not only designed to act as a deterrent for the trafficker but should allow for the confiscation of property and recovery of illegal cash flow. This should then be used as compensation for victims to make up for lost wages and psychological damage.

Investigations tend to need a nuanced approach and law enforcement requires training for this. This training may also need to be shared with judges and law schools and the handling of victims so as not to exacerbate victims' traumatic experiences.

While investigations are occurring the victims should be provided with a system of social support and residency permission should be considered on humanitarian grounds.

In the UK, cases of trafficking for sexual exploitation have been documented from 1999 by the Metropolitan Police, but no organisation existed to refer victims to for support and protection. It was also found that the law as it stood did not fit the offence of trafficking and prosecutions were typically for lower penalty offences, such as pimping. Also, due to the burden of proof required for higher penalty offences, conviction rates remained low between 1999 and 2003. However, there have been recent changes to bring legislation in line with the current knowledge of trafficking, e.g. the Sexual Offences Act 2003 was introduced to replace the Sexual Offences Act 1956.

Slavery and human trafficking can be tried under a wide range of legislation including:

Statute	Section	Description
Asylum and Immigration (Treatment of Claimants etc) Act 2004	4	Arrangement or facilitation of entry into the UK with the intention of exploiting them or with knowledge that someone else will exploit them.
Sexual Offences Act 2003	49	Controlling a child prostitute or a child involved in pornography.
Sexual Offences Act 2003	33	Causing a person, with a mental disorder impeding choice, to watch a sexual act
Sexual Offences Act 2003/1956	57	Trafficking into the UK for sexual exploitation
Sexual Offences Act 2003	58	Trafficking within the UK for sexual exploitation
Sexual Offences Act 1956	33(A)	Keeping or managing a brothel, or acting/ assisting in

		managing a brothel.
Criminal Law Act 1977	1	Conspiracy
Criminal Justice Act 2003	114	Admissibility of heresay evidence
Criminal Justice Act 2003	118	Preservation of certain common law categories of admissibility
Criminal Justice Act 2003	120	Other previous statements of witnesses
Criminal Justice Act 2003	121	Additional requirement of admissibility of multiple heresay
Criminal Justice Act 2003	126	Court's general discretion to exclude evidence.
Human Rights Act 1998	Art 6	Right to a fair trial
Council of Europe Convention on Action against Trafficking in Human Beings	Art 10	Identification of victims of trafficking

While all of these laws can be invoked for crimes involved in human trafficking, a specific purpose built bill is currently being debated through parliament called the Modern Day Slavery Bill. The aim of the bill is to:

- consolidate existing human trafficking and slavery offences to make the options available to law enforcement, when investigating and pursuing trafficking related charges, administratively simpler and operationally clearer;

-        increase the maximum sentence for human trafficking to life imprisonment, to ensure that modern-day slave drivers face the full force of the law;

-        introduce an anti-slavery commissioner to galvanise efforts in the UK to challenge modern slavery by working with government and law-enforcement agencies to realise more investigations, prosecutions and convictions of human traffickers;

-        introduce slavery and trafficking prevention orders and slavery and trafficking risk orders to restrict movements or impose other prohibitions on convicted or suspected traffickers to reduce the risk they pose; create a new requirement for 'first responders' to report all suspected cases of human trafficking to the national referral mechanism (NRM) - to improve understanding of the nature and scale of this crime and help improve the response.[1]

The Bill has been criticized somewhat, however, as failing to provide adequate protection to the victim – a necessary component in tackling slavery but

---

1

https://www.gov.uk/government/publications/draft-modern-slavery-bill

also as a human rights response. One example is the lack of action against changing the visa rules for migrant domestic workers. Domestic workers abroad that enter the country attached to the visas of migrant families can not change employers even if they are in abusive and exploitative situations. This is a point of contention and is currently being tackled by NGOs and advocacy groups.

UK Policy and Practices

Modern day slavery is getting increased attention from the media and from the Government. The fact that a bill is being drafted is considerable progress in targeting this crime. Criticism has included the lack of consideration to the actual victims. UK policy in a number of areas can directly or indirectly have an impact on victims or even contribute to the cause of modern day slavery.

Zero Hours Contracts

The global recession led to a 'race to the bottom' and demand for cheap goods and services. Some employers and employment agencies adopted zero hours contracts, which has been described as a post-modern form of slavery. A zero hours contract is a contract without guarantee of work, but demands obligations from the employee such as exclusivity. That means employees are waiting in limbo for work but may go days without any work.

This can make it hard for the 'employee' to live on the wages they eventually receive. Many argue these contracts should be illegal.

Sub-contracting

The larger an organisation grows, the more complex becomes their supply chains. Fragmented supply chains can include numerate intermediaries and forms of sub-contracting. Sub-contracting is perfectly legal although recommendations are for companies to pay special attention to their supply chains to ensure there are no signs of slavery within them.

More legal migration methods

The lack of legal migration methods into the UK mean that more and more people are seeking illegal methods making them vulnerable to trafficking and being held in slavery like conditions. A freer flow of people may naturally fill demand for low-skilled and cheap labour, although still according to minimum wage.

CONCLUSION

Modern day slavery is still rife in the present day and not in far-flung lands but on our doorstep. It is connected to deep-rooted social issues but is also a response to the economic climate of the day.
Whether exploitation is subtle or blatant, there are some common attributes to known cases:

- restriction of movement;
- intimidation;
- illegal status;
- no wages or wages below the minimum wage;
- physical or mental abuse.

Responses to modern day slavery are by and large done on an institutional level. Big players are responsible for tackling social and economic problems; social workers and other frontline staff will look at protecting victims; and law enforcement and the criminal justice system can prosecute perpetrators.

However, individuals can play a part too. The need for information raising isn't just necessary amongst the general public but applies in reverse also. Local police tend to respond to issues that the public are most concerned about. Complaints to the police about the prevalence of slavery will prompt law enforcement to take greater notice of susceptible areas. The public also influences policy and a letter to the local Member of Parliament can tip the balance on how the Government responds.

BIBLIOGRAPHY

Books
ALI, M. (2005) 'Treading Along a Treacherous Trail: Research on Trafficking in Persons in South Asia' in Data and Research on Human Trafficking: A Global Survey, edited by F. Laczko and E. Gozdziak (International Organisation for Migration: Geneva)

BALES, K. New Slavery: A Reference Handbook, ABC-CLIO: California 2004

BALES, K. Disposable People: New Slavery in the Global Economy, University of California Press: California 2004

CAMERON, S. and NEWMAN, E. (2007) 'Understanding Human Trafficking', in Trafficking in Humans, edited by S. Cameron and E. Newman (United Nations University:)

CHALLIS, J. and ELLIMAN, D. Child Workers Today, Quartermaine House Ltd: Sunbury 1979

GAATW 2001 Human Rights and Trafficking in Persons: A Handbook

MACDONALD, K. (2004) 'Using Documents' in: Researching Society and Culture edited by Clive Seale (Sage)

MARTENS, Global human smuggling : comparative perspectives / edited by David Kyle and Rey Koslowski (John Hopkins University Press: London; Baltimore 2005)

McCABE, K.A. Trafficking of Persons, Peter Lang Pub Inc: , 2008

MIKO, F.T. (2003) 'Trafficking in Women and Children: the US and International Response', in: Trafficking in Women and Children: Current Issues and Developments, edited by A.M. Troubnikoff (Nova, New York)

NAIM, M. Illicit: How smugglers, traffickers and copycats are hijacking the global economy, Doubleday: New York 2005

O'FICKENAUER, Global human smuggling: comparative perspectives / edited by David Kyle and Rey Koslowski (John Hopkins University Press: London; Baltimore 2005)

PETERSON, V.S. and PARISI, L. (1998) 'Are Women human? It's not an academic question', in: Human Rights fifty years on: A reappraisal, edited by T. Evans (Manchester University Press: Manchester)

ANDREAS, B. and VAN DER LINDEN, M (2005) 'Designing trafficking research from a labour market perspective: the ILO experience' in Data and Research on Human Trafficking: A Global Survey, edited by F. Laczko and E. Gozdziak (International Organisation for Migration: Geneva)
ZHANG Smuggling and Trafficking in Human Beings

Conference Papers
AFRUCA (2007) 'Modern Day Slavery of African Children in the UK: Addressing the Demand and Supply Nexus', Paper presented at an event to commemorate the 200th anniversary of the law abolishing the Trans-Atlantic slave trade, CMS Cameron McKenna LLP, London 25 – 26 July 2007
PEARSON, E. (2001) 'The need for effective witness protection in the prosecution of traffickers: a human rights framework for witness protection', Paper presented at the First Pan-African Regional Conference on Trafficking in Persons Abuja, Nigeria 19-23 February 2001

Journal Articles
ADAMS, N. (2003) Anti-trafficking legislation: protection or deportation? Feminist Review (2003) 73, 135–139

ANDERSON, B. and ANSRIJASEVIC (2009), R. Sex, slaves and citizens: the politics of anti-trafficking http://www.statewatch.org/news/2009/feb/soundings.pdf

BHABHA, J. (2004) Seeking Asylum Alone: Treatment of Separated and Trafficked Children in Need of Refugee Protection, International Migration Vol. 42 (1) 2004

CHASE, E. and STATHAM, J. (2005) Commercial and sexual exploitation of children and young people in the UK—a review, Child Abuse Review, Volume 14, Number 1, January 2005, pp. 4-25(22)

ENENAJOR, A. (2008) Rethinking Vulnerability: European Asylum Policy Harmonization and Unaccompanied Asylum Seeking Minors, Childhoods Today Volume 2 Issue 2 - December 23, 2008

HALLET, N. and others (2006) Lost without a Lawyer, Forced Migration Review Volume 25, May 2006, p.63

KANGSAPUNTA (2006)

KANTOLA, J. and SQUIRES, J (2004) Discourses Surrounding Prostitution Policies in the UK, European Journal of Women's Studies 2004; 11; 77

KELLY, L. (2003) The wrong debate: reflections on why force is not the key issue with respect to trafficking in women for sexual exploitation, Feminist Review 73 2003 139-144

LEE, E. (1966) A Theory of Migration, Demography, Vol.3, No.1 1966 47-57

SALT, J and STEINER J (1997) Migration as a business: the case of trafficking, International Migration, 35(4) 467-94

YOUNG, W. and QUICK, D. (2005) Combating Trafficking, Forced Migration Review Vol 25 41-42

People Trafficking: Upholding Rights and Understanding Vulnerabilities, Forced Migration Review Volume 25, May 2006

Government and Inter-Governmental Reports

CEOP (2009) Strategic Threat Assessment: Child Trafficking in the UK, Child Exploitation and Online Protection Centre, London, 2009

CEOP (2009) A scoping study into the outcomes for children and young people encountered in cannabis factories in the UK, Child Exploitation and Online Protection Centre, London, 2009

EUROPEAN COMMISSION (2004) Report of the Experts Group on Strategies for Combating the Trafficking of Women and Children (Brussels, 22 December 2004)

GAATW (2007) Response to the 24 January 2007 Report of the Special Rapporteur on the human rights aspects of the victims of trafficking in persons, especially women and children, Ms

Sigma Huda, HUMAN RIGHTS COUNCIL Fifth session Item 2 of the provisional agenda
HOME OFFICE (2000) Stopping Traffic: Exploring the extent of, and responses to, trafficking in women for sexual exploitation in the UK, Police Research Series Paper 125
HOME OFFICE (2007) Trafficking for the Purposes of Labour Exploitation: A literature Review, Online Report 10/07
HOME OFFICE (2007) UK Action Plan on Tackling Human Trafficking, (TSO Ref: 5545552)
HOUSE OF LORDS, HOUSE OF COMMONS JOINT COMMITTEE ON HUMAN RIGHTS, Human Trafficking: Twenty-sixth report of session 2005-2006, HL Paper 245–I HC 1127–I
LEHTI, M. (2003) Trafficking in woman and children in Europe, HEUNI, The European Institute for Crime Prevention and Control, affiliated with the United Nations, No.18 2003
MORRISON, J and CROSLAND, B. The trafficking and smuggling of refugees: the end game in European Asylum policy? UNHCR: Geneva, 2000.
MORRISSON, J. (2002) FMO Research Guide: Human Smuggling and Trafficking, Forced Migration Review Vol.11, October 2002
UNODC (2008) Human Trafficking: An Overview, United Nations: New York 2008
US DEPARTMENT OF STATE (2008) Trafficking in Persons Report

WELSH AFFAIRS COMMITTEE (2009)
Globalisation and Its Impact on Wales: Oral and
written evidence

NGO Reports
AMNESTY INTERNATIONAL, Joint NGO
Statement on the draft European Convention
against Trafficking in Human Beings
AMNESTY INTERNATIONAL (2008) Summary of
Amnesty International's Concerns in the Region,
July-December 2007, AI Index: EUR
01/001/2008
AMNESTY INTERNATIONAL (2008) UK: Briefing
to the Human Rights Committee, AI Index: EUR
45/011/2008

AMNESTY INTERNATIONAL (2008) United
Kingdom Submission to the UN Universal
Periodic Review, First session of the HRC UPR
Working Group, 7-18 April 2008
BAKHARI, F. (2009) Stolen Futures: Trafficking
for Forced Child Marriage in the UK, ECPAT UK,
2009
BEDDOE, C. (2007) Missing Out, ECPAT UK, 2007
BINDEL, J. (2006) No Escape? An Investigation
into London's Service Provision for Women
Involved in the Commercial Sex Industry,
POPPY-Project Eaves 2006

EAVES (2009) Of Human Bondage: Trafficking in women and contemporary slavery in the UK, Eaves Housing 2009

GUICHON, A and VAN DEN ANKER, C. (2006) Trafficking for Forced Labour in Europe: Report on a study in the UK, Ireland, the Czech Republic and Portugal. Anti-Slavery International: EU, 2006

KALAYAN (2008) The New Bonded Labour? The impact of proposed changes to the UK immigration system on migrant domestic workers, Oxfam and Kalayaan 2008

KAYE, M. (2003) The trafficking-migration nexus: combating trafficking through the protection of migrants' human rights, Anti-Slavery International, 2003

PEARSON, E. (2002) Human traffic, human rights: redefining victim protection, Anti-Slavery International 2002

SKRIVANKOVA, K. (2006) Trafficking for Forced Labour: UK Country Report, Anti-Slavery International 2006

SKRIVANKOVA, K. (2007) 'United Kingdom' in: Collateral Damage: The Impact of Anti-Trafficking Measures on Human Rights around the World, Global Alliance Against Traffic in Women 2007

SOMERSET, C. What the Professionals Know: The trafficking of children into and through the UK for sexual purposes, ECPAT UK, 2001.

SOMERSET, C. Cause for Concern? London social services and child trafficking, ECPAT UK, 2004
UNICEF (2003), Child Trafficking
http://www.unicef.org.uk/unicefuk/policies/policy_detail.asp?policy=7

Media
GUARDIAN (19 September 2007) 'Increased immigration boosts knife crime and drink-driving, police chief says'
http://www.guardian.co.uk/uk/2007/sep/19/immigration.immigrationandpublicservices
TELEGRAPH, (8 September 2014) 'Modern Slavery in Britain', '
http://www.telegraph.co.uk/sponsored/lifestyle/modern-slavery-britain/

Made in the USA
San Bernardino, CA
21 January 2018